PRINCE WILLIAM

First English edition published by Colour Library Books Ltd.
© 1984 Illustrations and text: Colour Library Books Ltd.,
  Guildford, Surrey, England.
This edition published by Greenwich House, a division of
  Arlington House, Inc., distributed by Crown Publishers, Inc.
h g f e d c b a
Display and text filmsetting by Acesetters Ltd.,
  Richmond, Surrey, England.
Color separations by Llovet, Barcelona, Spain.
Printed and bound in Barcelona, Spain.
by JISA-RIEUSSET and EUROBINDER.
ISBN 0 517 437988

Royal Heritage Series

PRINCE WILLIAM

Text by TREVOR HALL

Produced by Ted Smart and David Gibbon

GREENWICH HOUSE

'Aren't you fed up with having to answer questions about Prince William?', someone asked the Princess of Wales. Her reply was immediate, emphatic and affirmative, her look of mock impatience giving the only hint that perhaps she really rather enjoyed it all. Unlike almost every other mother, the Princess has had to come to terms with the fact that her son is everybody's baby, just as she herself has become international property. And come to tems with it she has, combining her own preference for personal privacy outside working hours with the insatiable public demand for news, and views, of the child to whom she may one day be obliged to pay homage as King.

Prince William was famous long before he was born. He received his first tribute from a damp-eyed Lord Mayor of London on that November day in 1981 when the Princess' pregnancy was announced. 'Babies are bits of stardust blown from the hand of God', he announced poetically amid a fever of rejoicing within London's Guildhall at the news. In the streets outside, less ethereal comments from the City's workforce congratulated Prince Charles on his manliness and good fortune, and on the speed of his achievement, for it had escaped no-one that it was barely three months since his marriage.

Popular reaction might not have been quite so forthright had the more 'decent' interval, traditionally observed by royalty, elapsed between that memorable royal wedding and the official announcement of the forthcoming birth. But the Prince and his wife were already scheduled to visit three Commonwealth countries in 1982, and it was imperative that prospective hosts should not spend time, money and effort on preparations for events which would now not materialise. But the early news meant that the Princess could not avoid having her weeks of morning sickness chronicled in almost intimate detail by the Press. 'Nobody told me it would be like this', she complained, and almost before the words had left her lips the newspapers were pressing Prince Charles for details. 'You all have wives', he replied, in an attempt to keep down the fuss, 'so you all know the problems'.

The problems in medical terms proved few. Immune to rubella, the Princess did not need special injections to protect her unborn child – just as well since she confesses to being terrified of needles – and the only brief alarm followed news that she had fallen down some stairs at Sandringham early in 1982. But there were difficulties of another sort: a non-stop barrage of Press speculation about every aspect of the forthcoming confinement. Most of it was well meant, if occasionally intrusive, though inevitably extremes proved irresistible. Photographs of the Princess sunbathing in her bikini in the Caribbean did nothing to make her pregnancy enjoyable.

When it really mattered, it was the Princess who caught the Press napping – almost literally. It was five in the morning when she arrived at St Mary's Hospital, Paddington, for her confinement, so the outcome of the long debate whether Britain's future King should or would be born within Palace walls or in a twelve-feet-square room in West London was resolved and acted on with not a photographer in sight. But neither Press nor people were slow to respond, and patient crowds waited in their thousands until the news was confirmed that the birth had been safely accomplished at just after nine o'clock that evening – Monday, 21st June, 1982 – the first day of summer.

Prince Charles emerged two hours after the birth to feverish congratulation, evidenced by two wide bands of lipstick to the right of his jaw, and pronounced his son 'beautiful' and 'in marvellous form', crying lustily and weighing seven pounds one and a half ounces. The blue eyes and fair, blondish hair, plus the fact that he was 58 per cent British – unlike his royal forebears for over three centuries – completed the dream. Everyone went away happy, even the Family Planning Association who said that the event could help reverse Britain's falling birth rate, and that 'Princess Diana could be to us what the electricity power blackout was to New York in 1965'. The following day, the crowds were there again to see Prince Charles, the Queen, Earl Spencer and Mrs Shand Kydd pay their respects before the baby and its proud parents left for Kensington Palace. The young Prince's public appearance less than twenty-four hours after his birth shattered another royal tradition, but it was a long time before he was seen again.

His names – William Arthur Philip Louis – were announced when he was a week old. William, Prince Charles confirmed that day, was a name that he and his wife liked and did not exist in the family at present. Arthur has been a frequent royal name since Queen Victoria's day, while Philip and Louis emphasise the strong Mountbatten influence in the family. 'No abbreviations please', said a Palace announcement, but in vain. Everything from 'Wee Willie Windsor' to 'Billy the Kid' has been tried, while the Press' nicknames – 'Prince of Wails', 'Prince of Wheels', 'Prince of Whales' and 'Prince of Wellies' – have reflected his behaviour, his transport, favourite toys and footwear respectively. His parents call him Wills.

His birth and full names were registered on the 19th July, when the Kensington registrar called at Kensington Palace. 'The ceremony was lovely', she said, 'and Prince Charles and the Princess of Wales were proud and happy'. Two weeks later he was christened. Prince Charles – well brought up to respect royal continuity – chose his grandmother Queen Elizabeth's 82nd birthday for the occasion, and that magnificent Victorian joined the other members of the immediate family at Buckingham Palace that day. Prince Andrew was prevented by exigencies in the Falklands, Princess Margaret by an Italian holiday, from being present. But it seemed the whole nation was there, spurred into involvement by the publication six days earlier of the first official photographs. Taken by Lord Snowdon, they showed an informal and relaxed couple fairly cocooning their pride and joy; Prince William looks quietly surprised at it all.

He was less silent as the Archbishop of Canterbury brought him into the Christian fold in the Palace's bow-windowed Music Room. William's repeated whimpers were welcomed as a token that the Devil had left his body, though all too soon were more correctly interpreted as the first signs of hunger. He yelled so loudly at the subsequent photo-call that the Queen Mother could only praise him for his healthy lungs, and the Queen for his early attempts at speechmaking. It was the Princess of Wales who, by putting the tip of her finger into his mouth, fooled him into silence until the session was over; and eventually he was driven back to Kensington Palace and the relative calm of his nursery. Most of his first six weeks had been spent there: a more pleasant spell of British weather than that which saw his birth assured him of several hours spent alfresco in the spanking new pram delivered by its South Wales manufacturers early that July. A low-slung, collapsible model, its cot is removable from the base – perfect for popping it into and out of the back of the car which takes him regularly to local parks and gardens for afternoon outings.

Prince William spent the first part of the following three months at Balmoral with his parents, and public sightings of him were necessarily rare. Prince Charles carried him in his carrycot off the plane that landed at Aberdeen early in August, and the growing baby was seen being wheeled in one of the Royal Family's older, coach-built, stand-by prams on the estate in mid-October. It was not till late that month that the Princess of Wales finally returned to London to resume her public engagements. Buckingham Palace agreed that one of the reasons for such a long stay was that she wanted to be near Prince William, although a full ten or twelve-week Balmoral break is par for the royal course. Prince William subsequently joined his parents at Kensington Palace during each week, with weekend breaks at Highgrove, their country home in Gloucestershire, where the accommodation is much more expansive. In addition to a night nursery and a bathroom, Prince William has a special day nursery decorated, on his mother's decision, with murals of fourteen Disney cartoon characters – a specially commissioned fantasy which took almost a month to complete.

The young Prince's seclusion agitated a public which already doted on him, and there were frequent demands in the ensuing months for more pictures of him. The eagle-eyed passer-by might have spotted him being carried by his nanny near Gatcombe Park in November, or being perambulated round Kensington Gardens in the following months, but it was not enough. Continued secrecy led to the belief that Prince William would feature in the Queen's Christmas television broadcast. One newspaper cleverly hedged its bets and insisted that he was included 'in the uncut version' of the recording. It turned out to be a prudent reservation.

Instead, there were two unexpected photo-calls at Kensington Palace just three days before Christmas, when television and still cameramen assembled in the Princess of Wales' pink and white first-floor study overlooking Kensington Palace Gardens. This unexpected event took place at her own suggestion, and she must have felt well rewarded by the success of it all. Her six-month-old son chortled and dribbled away without the ghost of a grumble, sucking his bright yellow teething-rattle and staring, fascinated, at the butterflies which decorated one of the cushions on the pink silk sofa. Diana made him grin by clicking her fingers and chatting to him, while Prince Charles had a crisp white handkerchief at the ready to mop up a sudden delivery of returned breakfast. 'I expect the baby experts will say we have handled him all wrong', he muttered wryly.

The following day, Prince William was ferried, bobble-hatted, with his parents to Windsor to spend Christmas with the Queen. Official comment on his behaviour in his first six months had been sparse, but already he had earned a reputation for making himself heard. The Queen's press officer's tactful admission back in July that 'he can be heard crying occasionally, but not very often' was amplified by Prince Charles at the christening – 'he gets noisier and angrier by the day'. Princess Diana let slip a comment which confirmed the impression, when she encountered a noisy baby during a visit to Dolgellau in November. But at least Prince William was sleeping through the night. By the end of September he was rarely waking up before six in the morning. 'That's a great relief', his mother told a housewife in Tooting shortly before Christmas.

Prince William surprised everyone from the beginning by his enormous appetite; 'he eats endlessly' his grandfather, Lord Spencer, told visitors to Althorp five weeks after his grandson was born. The Prince was breast-fed for the first two months of his life, by which time he had doubled his birth weight. By the end of November he weighed well over sixteen pounds and still, as Princess Diana told Sir Richard Attenborough, 'he never stops eating'. He was fairly well forward physically, having made a few gallant if unsuccessful attempts to stand up, though his mother had to admit in November that he was not even sitting up properly. 'I just can't wait for him to walk', she said during a visit to Cirencester.

Prince Charles was equally delighted with his son and heir. 'I am besotted with him', he had admitted. 'He's wonderful fun and really makes you laugh. He's not at all shy. He's a great grinner, but he does dribble a lot.' 'Just like his father', chipped in the Princess, who also revealed that her husband liked to bathe William. 'The things they pick up at his age', she added, horrified that at only five months he had already learned to spit.

Even at this early age, new horizons were opening up for young Prince William. Three weeks before Christmas it had been announced that he would accompany his parents on their six-week tour of Australia and New Zealand in the spring of 1983. The news ended weeks of speculation and advice on the subject, though confirmation that 'there was never any question of leaving him behind' did nothing to play down the endless rumour that Princess Diana had fought the Queen long and hard in order to get her way. Several reasons supporting both views were adduced, the hazard of two heirs to the throne travelling together being cited as a reason for his not going, while the psychological necessity of mother and baby being together as much as possible argued the other way. Very few, if any, commentators suggested probably the most cogent justification for Prince William's presence down-under, though with the prospective election of an Australian Prime Minister committed to the establishment of a Republic, the evidence was uncomfortably obvious. In a country where Republicanism flourishes so fiercely that even the Queen had stepped up the frequency of her visits there during the last five years, the showing of the young Prince to the Australians as a symbol of the monarchy's continuity was imperative. Had not Edward I done similarly almost exactly seven hundred years before as a stimulus to Welsh sympathy towards the English?

The Australians were well primed for Prince William's coming, not so much by a Buckingham Palace spokesman's promise that 'people will get plenty of chances to see him' – that proved wide of the mark – as by the details of the country estate at Woomargama where the Prince would stay during the Australian leg of the tour. He would occupy a small suite of rooms overlooking a paved courtyard and a swimming pool, safe and secluded in the 70-year-old homestead situated a mile from the nearest road and three from the nearest neighbours. Its proud owners, company director Leonard Darling and his wife, Margaret, promised to provide all the necessary nursery furniture – formerly used for their own grandchildren – and to convert a changing room beside the swimming pool into a playroom if necessary.

The excitement at being thus graced prompted the Australians to take a particular interest in a set of delightful photographs of the young Prince and his parents, taken in the Princess of Wales' sitting room at Kensington Palace in February, and released a few days before the tour began in March. 'The Commonwealth's heart', said one newspaper, 'is about to be seized forever by the tiny, curling fingers of a nine-month-old baby'. Sure enough, dressed in a white romper suit with blue smocking, there was Prince William, bigger and better than ever, chewing on a daffodil, playing with a toy koala and a large, rather amorphous teddy bear, and trying his hand at a few press-ups on a soft, quilted rug. The photographer, Tim Graham, enjoying only his second royal commission, admitted a few problems coaxing his subject into a photogenic frame of mind – 'He did cry a bit' – but the end result was a winner. You only had to look at the pictures to appreciate why the Prince and Princess were, after all, taking their son abroad.

Prince William travelled well. 'We heard him cry only twice in thirty hours', said an accompanying press secretary, adding that the baby's cot was accommodated in a cabin in which nanny Barbara Barnes also slept. On the day they arrived in Australia, he awoke at six o'clock and joined his parents for breakfast before the landing at Alice Springs two hours later. The crowds at the little airport were enormous, highly gratified by the honour of having the young Prince make his first Australian public appearance among them. Prince Charles was later to hope that 'a small portion of his impressionable subconscious will be filled with the sounds and smells of the real Australia', but his son's initial reaction to his new surroundings was more mundane. He yawned, blinked furiously in the fierce morning sunlight, and flinched as a large black fly smacked into his face. Then, with a swift kiss from his mother, he was taken back up the steps and into the aircraft to continue his journey to Woomargama, where his parents would join him after spending three days in Australia's Red Centre.

He was not seen again in public until the day before the Australian tour ended, but he was rarely out of the thoughts of either his parents or the public. After every stage of their tour, the Prince and Princess of Wales returned to Woomargama to stay overnight or even a whole weekend with their son. There was a special bonus at Easter when the family was together for four whole days in succession. In several of his official speeches, Prince Charles continually emphasised what it meant to him to have Prince William with him. 'I hope', he said in Sydney, 'he will grow to regard this country with affection and admiration'. Successive State Premiers took up the theme. In Adelaide the South Australian Premier hoped that 'Prince William's presence here will be the first of many visits', while Tasmania's Premier Gray went one better and looked forward 'to meeting Prince William and getting to know him and love him as much as we love you, Sir'.

Princess Diana revealed that her son was already getting 'a lot of affection from a lot of people', particularly during his first week when, unused to Australian time, he began waking up in the middle of the night. Fortunately the weather, disappointingly cool for the Australians, was not dissimilar from the English climate he had just left, and he adapted to it without difficulty. He was also the butt of his father's ready wit. At Hobart, Prince Charles referred to Tasmania's generous wedding present which, he said, 'ensured that our son was born with at least six silver spoons in his mouth. That's why we had to come here – to find out how to get them out.' At a Sydney reception his jokey revelation that Prince William was being fed at Woomargama on 'warm milk and minced kangaroo meat' backfired. Bombarded with protests from outraged do-gooders, he had to retreat a few days later: 'I was only attempting a joke. I thought Australians had a sense of humour'. Then, as a mischievous afterthought: 'In fact we bring him up on grass and beer'.

Prince William was no less a celebrity when the royal threesome arrived in New Zealand in mid-April. The Maoris called him *Tuakana*, or 'Heir' and made him a kiwi-feather cloak – a small-scale model of one they had already presented to his father. He stayed at the Governor-General's residence in Auckland, where a top-floor suite had been adapted to include a nursery brightly decorated with animal pictures and mobiles, and, since he was just on the threshold of his first crawl, fitted with a protective swing-gate at the top of the stairs. In his bedroom, which adjoined nanny Barnes' room, the curtains were lined with black material to keep out sunlight – an unnecessary precaution as the poor weather in New Zealand exceeded even Australia's drab climate. On the Prince's cot was a quilt appliquéd with pictures of children in colourful overalls and frocks, which a group of New Zealand women stitched to match the one they had sent to London at the time of his birth.

The highlight of his fortnight's stay was the eagerly awaited photo-call, which eventually took place on St George's Day. Facing manfully up to a posse of forty or fifty cameramen, Prince William set about exploring the secrets beneath the huge floral rug where he and his parents had established themselves on the lawn of their residence, and showed how well he had, finally, learned to crawl. Several times his mother and father had to grab him back to the centre of the rug, though not, on one occasion, before he had scooped up a handful of dirt and put it to his mouth. In between giving his wooden Bizzy Bee toy a great deal of his attention, he managed a few wobbly attempts at standing. It took less than fifteen minutes for all those not yet smitten by his charms to fall victim. Even the New Zealand government showed its appreciation by providing free disposable nappies, baby foods and toilet requisites in the Air New Zealand plane which took him back home! With him went the pick of over fifty thousand gifts from the people his parents met on their journeyings – everything from a boomerang made by a New South Wales champion to a kiwi whose beak opened to the sound of a Brahms lullaby.

Within six weeks his parents were on their foreign travels again – this time to Canada. Prince William did not go with them, on the grounds that, according to Prince Charles, 'life aboard *Britannia* might not have suited him. We feel that the ship's voyage would not be good for him'. Princess Diana missed him badly almost as soon as she touched down in Halifax, Nova Scotia, and said so promptly. It must have been enormous consolation for her – and she was clearly cheered by it – to receive scores of gifts to take back for him. There was a snow-suit from St Johns, a rocking horse from Prince Edward Island, a blue coat-of-arms sweater from Ottawa, and a replica fishing dory from the citizens of Shelburne. And only a week after their arrival, both the Princess and her husband got up very early to speak to Prince William on the telephone. It was his first birthday.

Prince Charles had to admit all he could hear on this occasion were 'a few little squeaks' but back home the celebrations cracked on apace. His parents had left just a few presents behind for Prince William to open on the day, and his morning was pleasantly interrupted by a pack of Brownies assembled outside Kensington Palace to sing *Happy Birthday To You*. Up in Birmingham, the city council threw a party for thirty babies who had been born on the same day as the young Prince, while in Croydon the Queen was overwhelmed with flowers, presents and messages of goodwill for her grandson.

He began walking in July, taking his first steps, uncertain but unaided, while at Highgrove. 'Now he is bigger and more active, I am sure more will be seen of him', a spokesman promised, but sadly it proved a forlorn hope. Only his comings and goings at airports while on his travels have been well enough documented to keep him in the public eye, and his first royal wave – at Aberdeen airport *en route* for London at the end of October 1983 – provided some celebrated photographs. The real reward for public patience came shortly before Christmas when, for the second successive year, and suggesting the setting of precedents, the Prince and Princess allowed their son to appear before a gaggle of twenty Press and television cameras. This took place in one of Kensington Palace's courtyards, where Prince William could be allowed to show off his walking skills with considerable freedom. As in New Zealand, he had to be hauled back into position – this time when he decided enough was enough and made for the gateway leading back to the Palace. His initial reluctance to perform again for the cameras suggested that he had inherited some of his mother's diffidence, but his eventual, charming and somewhat uncomprehending confrontation with the Pressmen reflected something of his father's genes.

His general good behaviour on that occasion was not taken as a sign that he had lost his capacity for upsetting things. In the previous few months, not content merely with dropping his father's golf balls into empty gumboots, climbing into wastepaper baskets or planting-tubs, or passing on to Prince Charles a virulent bug known as Respiratory Syncitial Virus, he had enlivened everybody's Balmoral holiday by setting off the Castle's security alarms, thus activating a well-rehearsed internal security drill and putting Aberdeen police station on full alert.

It was the sort of thing from which everyone emerged looking rather foolish, except for the malefactor himself, who escaped condemnation under the rule which expects boys to be boys. He may have appeared rather grave and serious at times: 'We tried everything to get a smile out of him', said one of the staff looking after him in Auckland, 'but he just looked down at us very seriously as if to remind us of our place'. But no one wants him to grow up without at least a touch of mischief. Remembering that even the solemn and dutiful Prince Charles was once scandalously involved with a glass of cherry brandy, Prince William's admiring public will continue to indulge his peccadillos for a long time to come, as it follows his childhood with as much goodwill as curiosity.

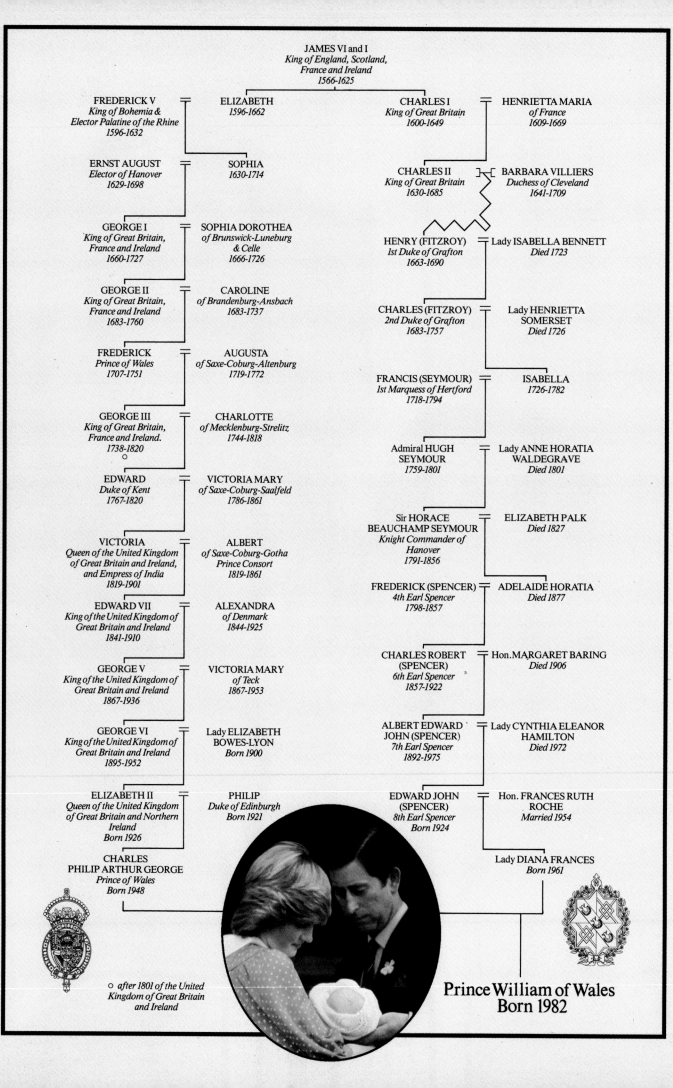

JAMES VI and I
King of England, Scotland, France and Ireland
1566-1625

FREDERICK V
King of Bohemia & Elector Palatine of the Rhine
1596-1632

ELIZABETH
1596-1662

CHARLES I
King of Great Britain
1600-1649

HENRIETTA MARIA
of France
1609-1669

ERNST AUGUST
Elector of Hanover
1629-1698

SOPHIA
1630-1714

CHARLES II
King of Great Britain
1630-1685

BARBARA VILLIERS
Duchess of Cleveland
1641-1709

GEORGE I
King of Great Britain, France and Ireland
1660-1727

SOPHIA DOROTHEA
of Brunswick-Luneburg & Celle
1666-1726

HENRY (FITZROY)
1st Duke of Grafton
1663-1690

Lady ISABELLA BENNETT
Died 1723

GEORGE II
King of Great Britain, France and Ireland
1683-1760

CAROLINE
of Brandenburg-Ansbach
1683-1737

CHARLES (FITZROY)
2nd Duke of Grafton
1683-1757

Lady HENRIETTA SOMERSET
Died 1726

FREDERICK
Prince of Wales
1707-1751

AUGUSTA
of Saxe-Coburg-Altenburg
1719-1772

FRANCIS (SEYMOUR)
1st Marquess of Hertford
1718-1794

ISABELLA
1726-1782

GEORGE III
King of Great Britain, France and Ireland.
1738-1820
○

CHARLOTTE
of Mecklenburg-Strelitz
1744-1818

Admiral HUGH SEYMOUR
1759-1801

Lady ANNE HORATIA WALDEGRAVE
Died 1801

EDWARD
Duke of Kent
1767-1820

VICTORIA MARY
of Saxe-Coburg-Saalfeld
1786-1861

Sir HORACE BEAUCHAMP SEYMOUR
Knight Commander of Hanover
1791-1856

ELIZABETH PALK
Died 1827

VICTORIA
Queen of the United Kingdom of Great Britain and Ireland, and Empress of India
1819-1901

ALBERT
of Saxe-Coburg-Gotha Prince Consort
1819-1861

FREDERICK (SPENCER)
4th Earl Spencer
1798-1857

ADELAIDE HORATIA
Died 1877

EDWARD VII
King of the United Kingdom of Great Britain and Ireland
1841-1910

ALEXANDRA
of Denmark
1844-1925

CHARLES ROBERT (SPENCER)
6th Earl Spencer
1857-1922

Hon. MARGARET BARING
Died 1906

GEORGE V
King of the United Kingdom of Great Britain and Ireland
1867-1936

VICTORIA MARY
of Teck
1867-1953

ALBERT EDWARD JOHN (SPENCER)
7th Earl Spencer
1892-1975

Lady CYNTHIA ELEANOR HAMILTON
Died 1972

GEORGE VI
King of the United Kingdom of Great Britain and Ireland
1895-1952

Lady ELIZABETH BOWES-LYON
Born 1900

ELIZABETH II
Queen of the United Kingdom of Great Britain and Northern Ireland
Born 1926

PHILIP
Duke of Edinburgh
Born 1921

EDWARD JOHN (SPENCER)
8th Earl Spencer
Born 1924

Hon. FRANCES RUTH ROCHE
Married 1954

CHARLES PHILIP ARTHUR GEORGE
Prince of Wales
Born 1948

Lady DIANA FRANCES
Born 1961

○ *after 1801 of the United Kingdom of Great Britain and Ireland*

Prince William of Wales
Born 1982

The keynote of Diana's pregnancy was enjoyment, and a willingness to be seen in public (above and overleaf, left). Now, (opposite and overleaf, right) Diana enjoys motherhood too.

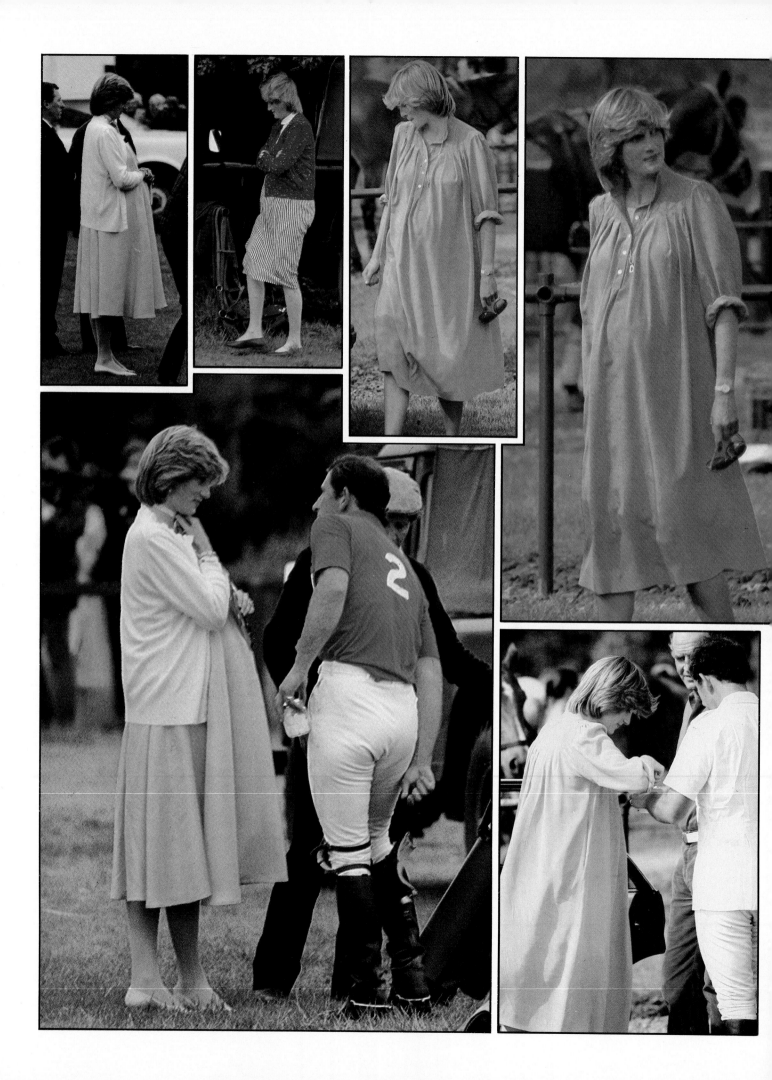

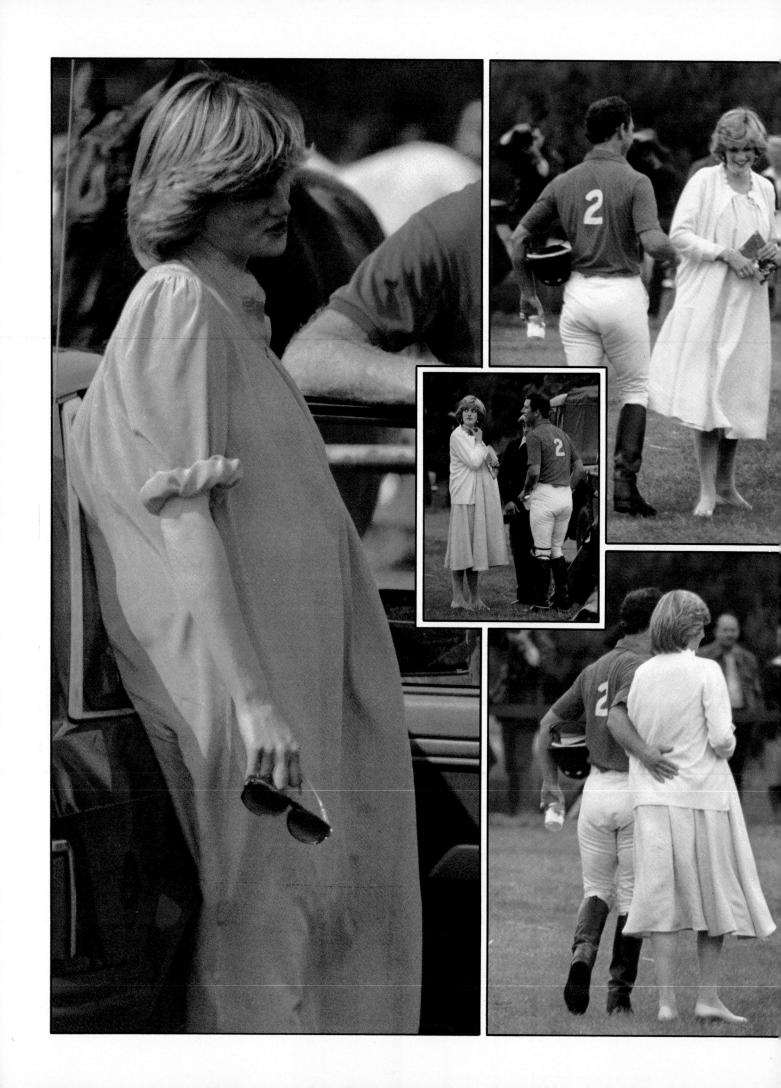

Scotching rumours that she disliked the sport, Diana watched Charles play polo several times during the final weeks of her pregnancy. The last time was five days before William's birth.

Days were never so busy at the Lindo Wing of St Mary's Hospital, Paddington, as on 21st and 22nd June, 1982. The news that Diana had gone into hospital brought a rush of spectators to the street, and a flood of tributes to the door. Prince Charles emerged two hours after William's birth, jubilantly responsive to a thousand cheers and good wishes. The following day, the Queen and Earl Spencer were among the newborn's first visitors. (Right) nothing special about William's birth certificate – except a rash of princely names.

| NHS Number LSBSS 115 | **BIRTH** | Entry No. **115** |

| Registration district | Westminster | Administrative area |
| Sub-district | Westminster | City of Westminster |

CHILD

1. Date and place of birth: Twenty first June 1982 St. Mary's Hospital Praed Street Westminster

2. Name and surname: His Royal Highness Prince William Arthur Philip Louis

3. Sex: Male

FATHER

4. Name and surname: His Royal Highness Prince Charles Philip Arthur George Prince of Wales

5. Place of birth: Westminster

6. Occupation: Prince of the United Kingdom

MOTHER

7. Name and surname: Her Royal Highness The Princess of Wales

8. Place of birth: Sandringham Norfolk

9.(a) Maiden surname: SPENCER

(b) Surname at marriage if different from maiden surname: —

10. Usual address (if different from place of child's birth): Highgrove Near Tetbury Gloucestershire

INFORMANT

11. Name and surname (if not the mother or father): —

12. Qualification: Father

13. Usual address (if different from that in 10 above): —

14. I certify that the particulars entered above are true to the best of my knowledge and belief

Charles .... Signature of informant

15. Date of registration: Nineteenth July 1982

16. Signature of registrar: Joan V. Webb Registrar

17. Name given after registration, and surname:

The public showing of a future king on the very day after his birth was a timely breach of yet another royal tradition. A nation accustomed to waiting several weeks for the privilege of seeing a new royal baby was delighted when Diana stepped out of the hospital and received her eighteen-hour-old son from Prince Charles. Then it was back home to Kensington Palace, where mother and baby could enjoy a few weeks privacy.

Speculation as to the new baby's name was already under way, with newspaper and magazine competitions vying with hastily-organized sweepstakes in offices and other places of work throughout the country. Among the more outlandish suggestions were Ronald, after Ron Greenwood, the manager of an England football team then well on its way in the World Cup competition; and Stanley, after the capital of the Falkland Islands which had been liberated only a week before the royal birth.

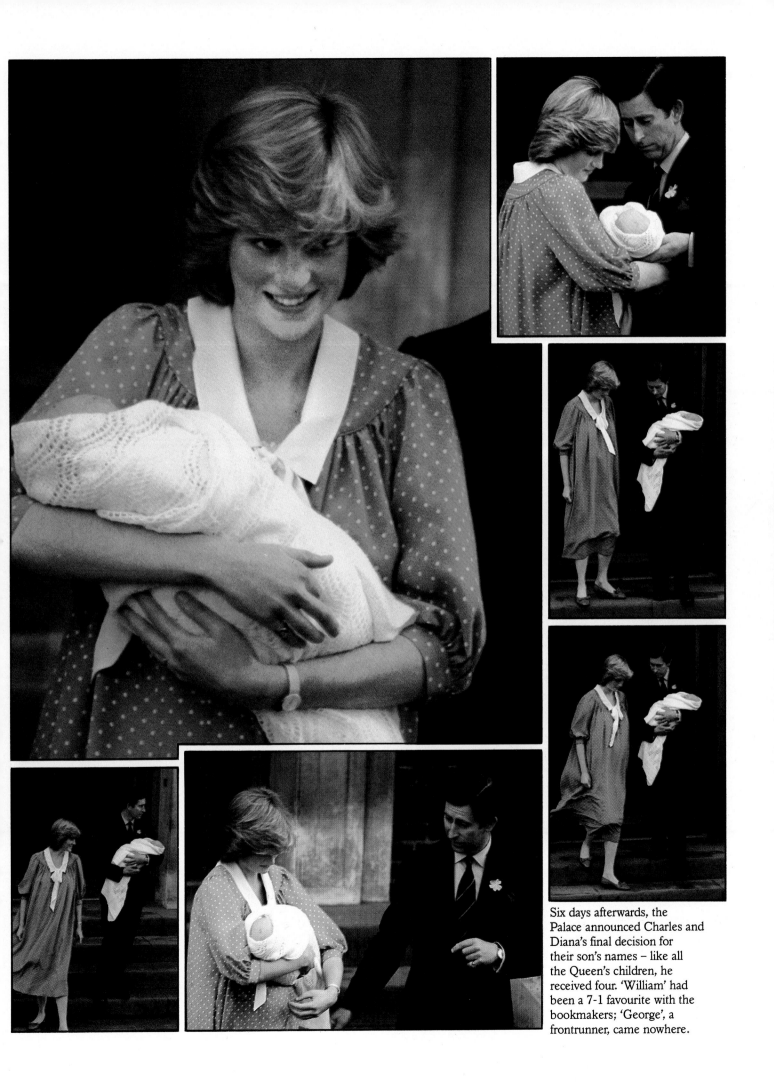

Six days afterwards, the Palace announced Charles and Diana's final decision for their son's names – like all the Queen's children, he received four. 'William' had been a 7-1 favourite with the bookmakers; 'George', a frontrunner, came nowhere.

(Far right) William's deliverer, gynaecologist George Pinker, and his nanny, Barbara Barnes. William's christening was, by royal standards, a private affair. Among sixty guests were Countess Spencer and six

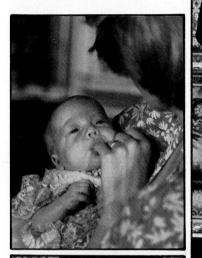

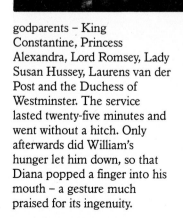

godparents – King Constantine, Princess Alexandra, Lord Romsey, Lady Susan Hussey, Laurens van der Post and the Duchess of Westminster. The service lasted twenty-five minutes and went without a hitch. Only afterwards did William's hunger let him down, so that Diana popped a finger into his mouth – a gesture much praised for its ingenuity.

Diana was seen only rarely for the remainder of that summer, and the following autumn was spoiled for her by the persistent rumours that, in her attempts to regain her shape after Prince William's birth, she had come close to contracting anorexia nervosa the slimmers' disease which her sister Sarah had suffered some years before. The rumours were disproved and the following spring and summer saw Diana at her best – slim,

chic and confident, both on official duties and on her many private visits to the polo fields. Even her original going-away outfit was being worn again with ease (opposite page) – some say it had been adjusted to cope with her much slimmer figure.

So effectively had Diana 'minded her figure', as she once put it, that she bought a whole new wardrobe of day dresses and evening gowns (pictures right and bottom) to complement those she had worn long before William was born (pictures far right). Jaunty pedal pushers (below) created something of a precedent, and probably helped to make her

'the most influential dresser' of 1983. But it was William whom everyone wanted to see, and demands for more pictures secured a set of delightful studies taken just before his first Christmas in 1982 (opposite page).

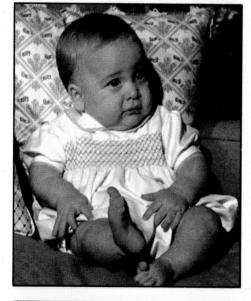

Fashion pundits scorned William's 'old-fashioned' rompers on this occasion, but demand for them leapt almost overnight – so much so that one Derbyshire factory reopened after seventeen months, to manufacture them.

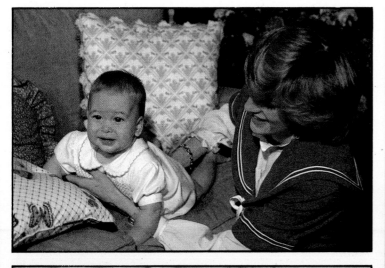

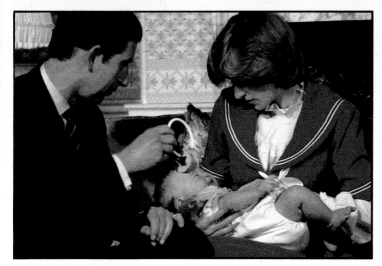

A fortnight before, it was announced that William would accompany his parents to Australia and New Zealand. The decision thrilled the old Dominions, though he was rarely seen in either country. In Australia, for instance, only his first day – in Alice Springs (centre) – and his last – in Melbourne (above) – brought public appearances. On that last occasion he looked healthy and even bronzed, despite the indifferent weather.

One newspaper reader protested at what she called the folly of allowing Prince William out into such fierce sunlight at Alice Springs (bottom picture) without a hat on, but it didn't seem to cause the young visitor any lasting harm. Nanny Barnes, who brought

William off the plane for a brief showing to a vast welcoming crowd (left), accompanied him onward to home base at Woomargama, while his parents carried out their dazzlingly-successful tour. (Right) the royal couple at a dinner-dance in Sydney.

The first pictures of Prince William in Alice Springs (below centre) were flashed around the whole country, serving as a substitute for the real thing as Charles and

Diana travelled from state to state by themselves. Rarely was William forgotten – either in official speeches of welcome, or in chance conversations between Diana and her thousands of admirers – but at no time until the end of the Australian leg of the tour was Prince William seen again in public (opposite page).

Though looking a little bemused on arrival in Australia (below), William seemed to cope pretty well. Babies, one doctor assured an anxious public, do not suffer from jet lag, because their

encountered will be that inside Prince William'! One paediatrician confirmed that babies coped with extremes of heat better than most adults – but that proved not to be a problem. Indeed, William soon acquired a reputation as a rainmaker. His arrival at Woomargama coincided with the first rain in the area for four years, and rain followed

lives centre around food rather than sleeping patterns. Nevertheless, dehydration was likely to occur, so extra fluids were necessary during the flight. And the risk of

turbulent weather, coupled with the knowledge that changes in pressure might upset the digestive system, led one observer to hope that 'the only strong wind

his parents to almost every corner of the country thereafter. Even Melbourne was uncharacteristically cool and windy on the eve of their departure (left and above).

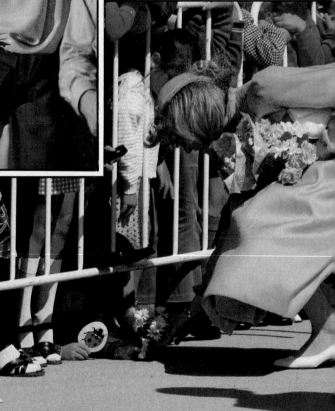

William became the topic of conversation everywhere, and Diana's encounters with children (above right) emphasised the common interest. *Punch* magazine brought the link wider 'when he's not drinking he's either throwing up or crawling around on all fours looking for his other shoe', ran one cartoon caption. 'No wonder the Australians love him.' One local publican was unimpressed: 'Prince William?' he said. 'What race is that in?'

The sight of nanny Barnes carrying William about left Diana open to some criticism. 'The royal couple only play at parenthood, while underlings provide the real care,' wrote one newspaper. Nevertheless, Billy the Kid, as Australians affectionately nicknamed him, had certainly enhanced his parents' popularity.

William did his parents proud
when they presented him before
the photographers in Auckland.
He showed no sign of the
petulance his father had once
accused him of, and every sign
that the exploring traditions
for which down under is famous
were far from dead. And we all
learned for the first time
that the family call him
'Wills'.

and accepted a magnificent garland from them (bottom picture). Towards the end of the tour she accompanied Prince Charles to Waitangi (below), where the Maoris first ceded sovereignty to the British Crown in 1840. Here she received a jade necklace symbolising fertility, and joined in the old custom whereby visitors of esteem are ferried in beautifully-carved Maori canoes across the Bay of Waters – an expedition which

With William established at Government House in Auckland throughout the tour, the limelight was very much on his mother as, for the first time, she came face to face with Maori customs. Almost literally, in fact, as on the first full day she executed her first *hongy*, or pressing of noses, with representatives of the local Maori community proved rather more hazardous in mid-passage than had been expected (far left). Though they never met him, the Maoris offered Prince William a cloak of kiwi feathers and called him Tuakana-Heir.

Like his mother, Prince William caused something of an upset in the fashion world. Following pictures like these (below and below left), rompers for toddlers began to replace T-shirts and short trousers. 'Prince William has changed baby fashions overnight', said the managing director of one firm of children's clothes manufacturers. One British newspaper offered a similar

romper suit to each of the first ten readers to send in correct answers to a simple royal competition. Meanwhile, the perennial question, 'Whom does he take after?', seemed to be resolved in favour of Lord Spencer, with a bit of Prince Charles thrown in. The staff at Government House in Auckland certainly thought he had more than a touch of royalty and aristocracy about him!

William's first public display of crawling (bottom pictures) made hot news, but despite some attempts at standing on his own two feet (below) he wasn't able to perfect a solo performance on this occasion, and learning to walk took another three months. The multicoloured toy bee which his parents brought along for the photo session wasn't his favourite; Princess Diana had disclosed the previous month that at home he prefers a plastic whale which shoots

little balls out of the top of its head. She also mentioned that he would one day ride a Shetland pony – and it was at about this time that the Shetland Pony Stud Society gave William a pony called Lion, which is being broken in and trained in Leicestershire. Lion will be transferred to the royal stables in due course, when William – sometime after his second birthday – follows his cousin Peter Phillips and begins to learn to ride.

Two triumphal Commonwealth tours renewed the demands upon Diana at home and she more than justified the regular cliché 'radiant' that summer. In Canada (top left) she missed William, particularly as they were apart on his first birthday. 'I can't tell you what present we will be getting him,' said Charles, 'but it will be something he won't be able to break.' William had already attracted a reputation for being perhaps a little too vigorous!

Maintaining William's privacy meant no more official pictures for eight months. But the photographers found that his mother more than made up for that.

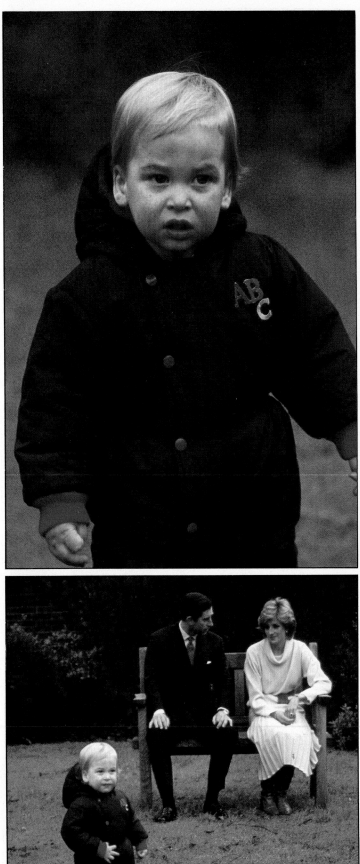

In December William, now over two stone and almost three feet tall, met the Press in the garden of Kensington Palace. Independent as ever, he left his parents to size up the posse of photographers – then decided he'd had enough, and made for home. Fortunately, Charles persuaded him back.

Princess' pregnancy. Not for the first time, the royal watchers' thunder had been stolen, and they barely disguised their chagrin. Charles and Diana were delighted, as were the Queen, Earl Spencer and others.

Summer 1983 was a time of growing speculation that Diana might be expecting her second child. Several casual remarks by the royal couple proved too tempting for the Press to ignore and there was much talk of 'William's brother or sister'. The news that Charles and Diana would visit Italy in October 1984 effectively dampened the rumours, but in February came the news of its postponement – owing to the

The news of Diana's pregnancy was suppressed during her January skiing trip to Liechtenstein and, by an arrangement with the Press, she was left in peace for most of her holiday.

As with all Charles and Diana's short holidays abroad, William did not accompany them to Liechtenstein. He remained at Sandringham with the Queen, who warmed to this rare opportunity of looking after her grandson.

Britain's youngest Royal Family: a typical sequence of pictures, taken at the beginning of their 1983 Balmoral holiday. Though William has learned to wave to those who watch his comings and goings, he has no means of knowing why he attracts large crowds, far less of suspecting his daunting destiny. His parents are determined to preserve him from undue publicity, preventing healthy public curiosity from becoming obsessive or vulgar. Though he will of course remain second in line of accession to the throne, William will shortly experience a few subtle changes when his brother or sister arrives. His reaction may well tell us more about what sort of person he will grow up to be.